better together*

*This book is best read together, grownup and kid.

 akidsco.com

○ **a**

○ **kids**

○ **book**

● **about**

Tests

by Missi Thurman

A Kids Co.
Editor Jelani Memory
Designer Rick DeLucco
Creative Director Rick DeLucco
Studio Manager Kenya Feldes
Sales Director Melanie Wilkins
Head of Books Jennifer Goldstein
CEO and Founder Jelani Memory

DK
Senior Production Editor Jennifer Murray
Senior Production Controller Louise Minihane
Senior Acquisitions Editor Katy Flint
Acquisitions Project Editor Sara Forster
Managing Art Editor Vicky Short
Managing Director, Licensing Mark Searle

First American edition, 2025
Published in the United States by DK Publishing, 1745 Broadway, 20th Floor,
New York, NY 10019

First published in Great Britain in 2025 by
Dorling Kindersley Limited, 20 Vauxhall Bridge Road, London SW1V 2SA
A Penguin Random House Company

The authorised representative in the EEA is
Dorling Kindersley Verlag GmbH. Arnulfstr. 124, 80636 Munich, Germany

A catalog record for this book is available from the Library of Congress.
A CIP catalogue record for this book is available from the British Library.
ISBN: 978-0-2417-4330-0

DK books are available at special discounts when purchased in bulk for sales
promotions, premiums, fund-raising, or education use. For details, contact:
DK Publishing Special Markets, 1745 Broadway, 20th Floor, New York, NY 10019
SpecialSales@dk.com

Printed and bound in China
www.dk.com
akidsco.com

MIX
Paper | Supporting
responsible forestry
FSC™ C018179

This book was made with Forest
Stewardship Council™ certified
paper – one small step in DK's
commitment to a sustainable future.
Learn more at **www.dk.com/uk/
information/sustainability**

To students: I see how hard you are working. Be proud of yourselves and your ability to do hard things. You deserve the best and I apologize for times when we as educators didn't meet your needs or recognize your gifts. Within you lies an endless potential to learn, grow, and shape the world.

To educators: I see you and the hard-fought battles both won and lost on the pendulum of testing and assessment. Your commitment to loving and teaching children well is everything. Thank you for continuing to show up, and know that your efforts, often unseen and unspoken, resonate beyond the classroom walls.

Intro
for grownups

Testing is a topic that brings out BIG feelings from almost everyone. Even though it's been several years since most grownups took a test, many still recall their own experiences—good, bad, or otherwise.

The anxiety and pressure that kids often feel around testing means tests rarely give us an accurate picture of their knowledge and skills. Testing isn't supposed to just be about right or wrong answers; it's about growing. BUT, that only happens if we set kids up for success by understanding testing's true purpose and use.

This book explores how testing has changed and how teachers and students can work as a team to approach testing with agency and curiosity. After all, every kid's brain is full of amazing things—if only we could take a peek inside!

So, let's turn the page and dive into the world of testing together. Are you ready? Let's go!

What do you already know about tests?

When you think about taking a test, lots of words and feelings might pop into your brain.

Nervousness, Anxiety, Fear, Excitement, Dread, Hope, Avoidance, A, B, C, D, F, 1, 2, 3, 4, 5, Aced, Proficient, Meets, Pass/Fail, Flunked, Nailed it!

The grownups in your life probably have a lot of thoughts about tests, too.

They might be the same or different than how you feel.

They might be thinking...

Success, Failure, Future, Now, Happy Life, Good College, Did better than I did!

News flash:

TESTING HAS

CHANGED!

why?

Because *teachers are learning* how to do it better.

In the past, the information produced from tests wasn't as helpful as it is today.

Now, teachers often use **assessments** instead of tests (even if they still call them tests).

"Assessments" can also be...

- ○ progress monitors
- ○ quizzes
- ○ exams
- ○ papers
- ○ reports
- ○ speeches
- ○ unit tests
- ○ finals
- ○ midterms

Assessments are a way to show teachers what you know, what you are able to do, what you have learned...

annnnnd

what you still need to learn.

This means

it's not
to pass

possible or fail.

If you get a question right, your teacher knows you're ready for more challenges.

If you get a question wrong,
your teacher knows to try a new
approach to help you learn.

Do you ever wonder what happens to your assessment after you turn it in?

Well, the questions you've answered are like a big

treasure hunt

for your teacher.

Teachers are responsible for making sure kids get what they need to be successful.

So, when they look at answers from an assessment, that's where the **treasure** is.

They help your teachers...

make
a plan.

Let's say you take an
assessment on math.

Your teacher then looks at the questions you got right or wrong.

They think about the things you've said and the work you've done in class.

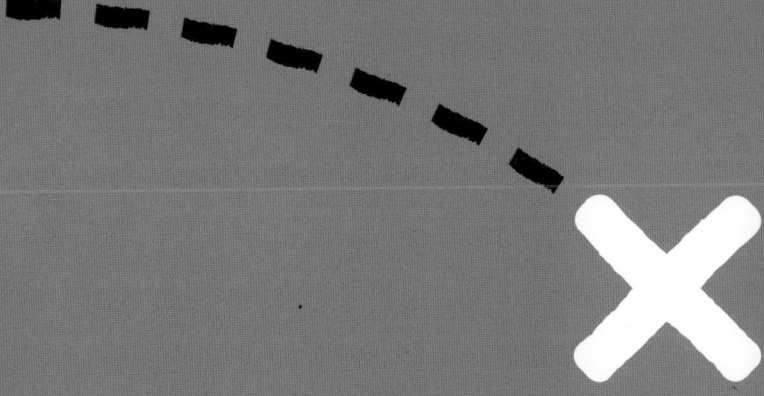

And using that as a guide, they make a plan for what they are going to teach next and how to best teach it.

Because kids learn in different ways,
teachers work together to make plans
for the unique needs of each student.

Sometimes, that lesson is with the whole class, and sometimes, those lessons take place in smaller groups.

They're both

od!

If you feel anxious or nervous when you think about taking an assessment, take a deep breath and remind yourself that you are a hard worker who gives their best effort!

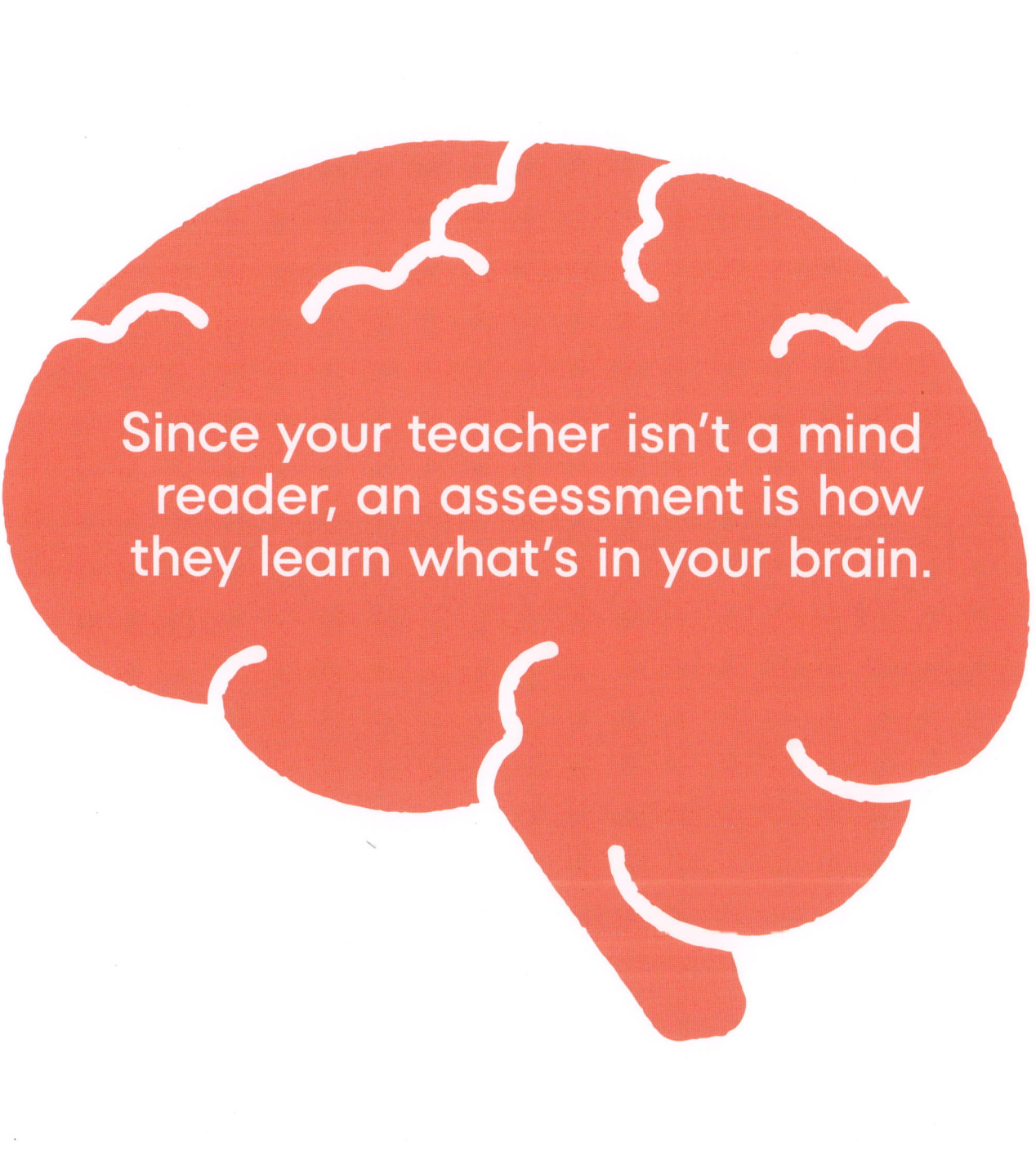

Since your teacher isn't a mind reader, an assessment is how they learn what's in your brain.

A paper-and-pencil assessment is only 1 of the ways they can figure this out.

They are always looking
for those treasures...

during class, when you're talking with your teacher, discussing with others, and in the work that you do.

The magic really happens when they put all of the pieces together.

It's kind of like a puzzle.

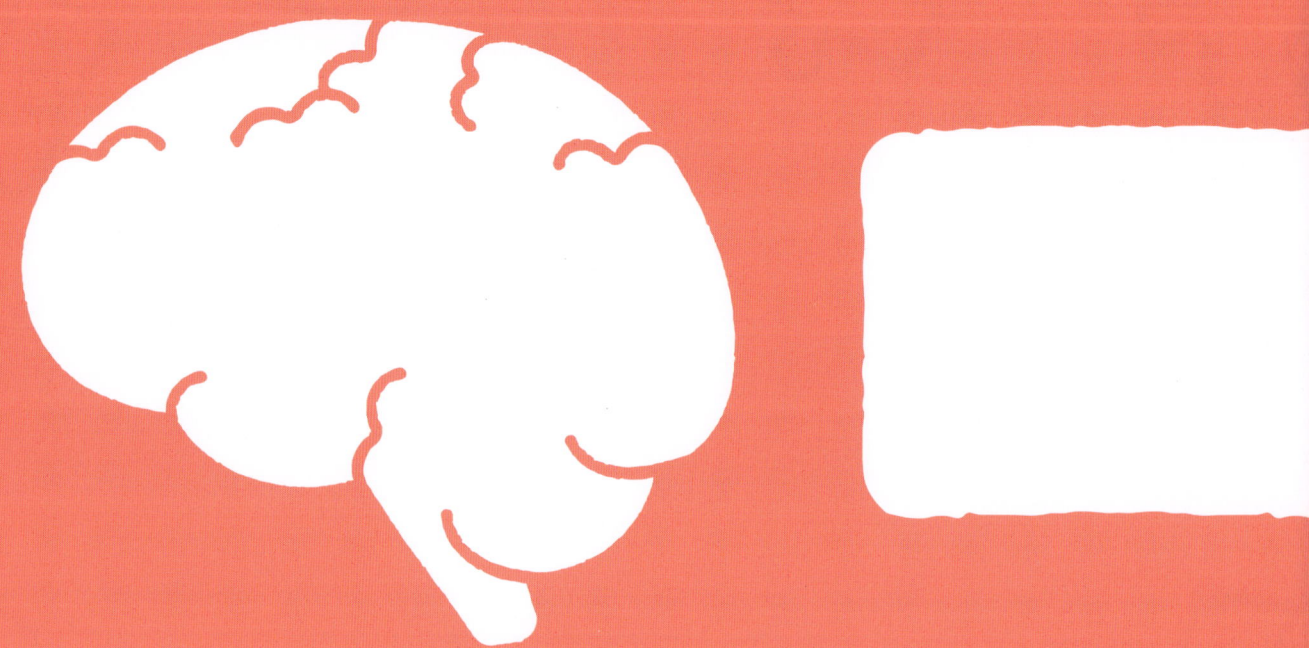

When you take an assessment, your job is to share what you've learned and what **YOU** know.

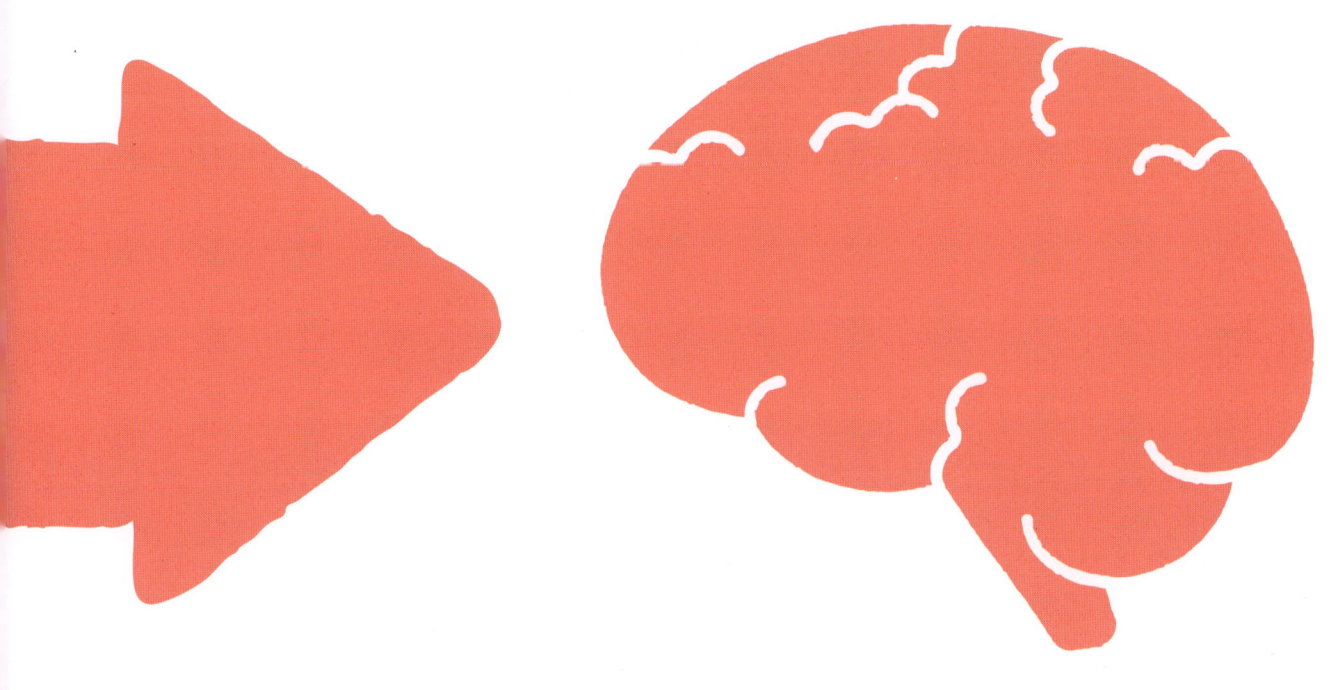

If you don't know or feel confused,
your teacher wants to know that, too.

What part was confusing? Which word was hard? Where did you get stuck?

It's good to know what you *do* know and what you *don't* know •••••••••

..................yet.

This information helps you and your teacher work as a

team!

So, no matter what, just do your best! Know that learning, making mistakes, getting feedback, and trying again are **all** part of what success looks like.

And that's true now, and
even when you're a grownup.

Oh, and 1 more little thing...

It's important to know that assessments CAN't reveal everything about you.

Your reading assessment won't tell us that you are a fierce athlete, and your math assessment doesn't show us that you are an amazing artist and a loyal friend.

There are many parts of you that others learn simply by being around you and how you make them feel.

And these the most
things of

are
important
all.

Outro
for grownups

ur journey doesn't end here! For the amazing grownups reading this with incredible kids, here's how to keep the dialogue going:

1. Prioritize listening to your student over sharing your own experiences. Embrace the idea that testing can be done differently (and better) than it was for you. Testing is evolving, but the experience for kids won't change if our language and attitudes about them don't!

2. Have open conversations about how teachers will use the information. Hint: Wrong answers often give us more insight than right ones!

3. Encourage a growth mindset by celebrating effort and progress, not just high scores.

4. Stay in touch with teachers. Understand the purpose of assessments and how you can support your student's learning at home. Don't be afraid to advocate for accommodations that they may need.

Let's turn the page on testing anxiety and open a new chapter where assessment is just one of many tools that help us learn about the wondrous world inside our kids' minds.

About The Author

Missi Thurman (she/her) wrote this book for her students, past and present. Today, she works with school districts and teaches them about the exciting science of learning. Every day, Missi observes educators working hard to plan thoughtfully and use data to make better decisions for their kids, but there are some barriers. The test-taking environment doesn't support every kid's ability to demonstrate what they know—some kids find it hard to try their best, and others worry too much about being perfect.

Missi wrote this book to offer kids a sneak peek into the "secret" world of what teachers do before and after school with their students' work! Her hope is that it reduces the mysterious testing scaries and helps kids, their grownups, and their teachers become better partners in helping every student succeed.

 @missmissthurman   🌐 educationalexcellence.org

Made to empower.

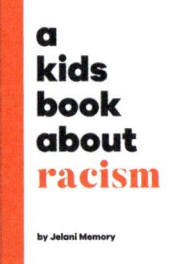
a kids book about **racism**
by Jelani Memory

a kids book about ANXIETY
by Ross Szabo

a kids book about DISABILITY
by Kristine Napper

a kids book about IMAGINATION
by LEVAR BURTON

a kids book about belonging
by Kevin Carroll

a kids book about fail**y**ure
by Dr. Laymon Hicks

a kids book about GRATITUDE
by Ben Kenyon

a kids book about LIFE ONLINE
by Dave S. Anderson & Blake Fleischacker

a kids book about body image
by Rebecca Alexander

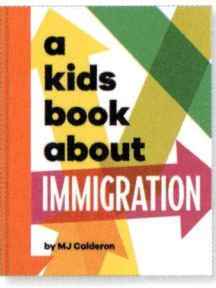
a kids book about IMMIGRATION
by MJ Calderon

a kids book about EMPATHY
by Daron K. Roberts

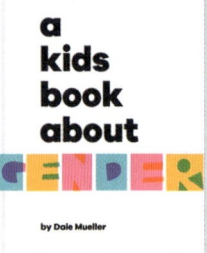
a kids book about GENDER
by Dale Mueller

a kids book about Love
by ZIGGY MARLEY

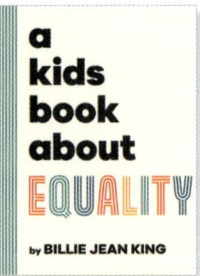
a kids book about EQUALITY
by BILLIE JEAN KING

a kids book about MONEY
by Adam Stramwasser

a kids book about FEMINISM
by Emma Mcilroy

a kids book about adventure
by Dr. Ben Tertin

a kids book about CLIMATE CHANGE
by Zanagee Artis Olivia Greenspan

a kids book about CONFIDENCE
by Joy Cho

a kids book about BEING NONBINARY
by Hunter Chinn-Raicht
in partnership with The GenderCool Project

Discover more at akidsco.com